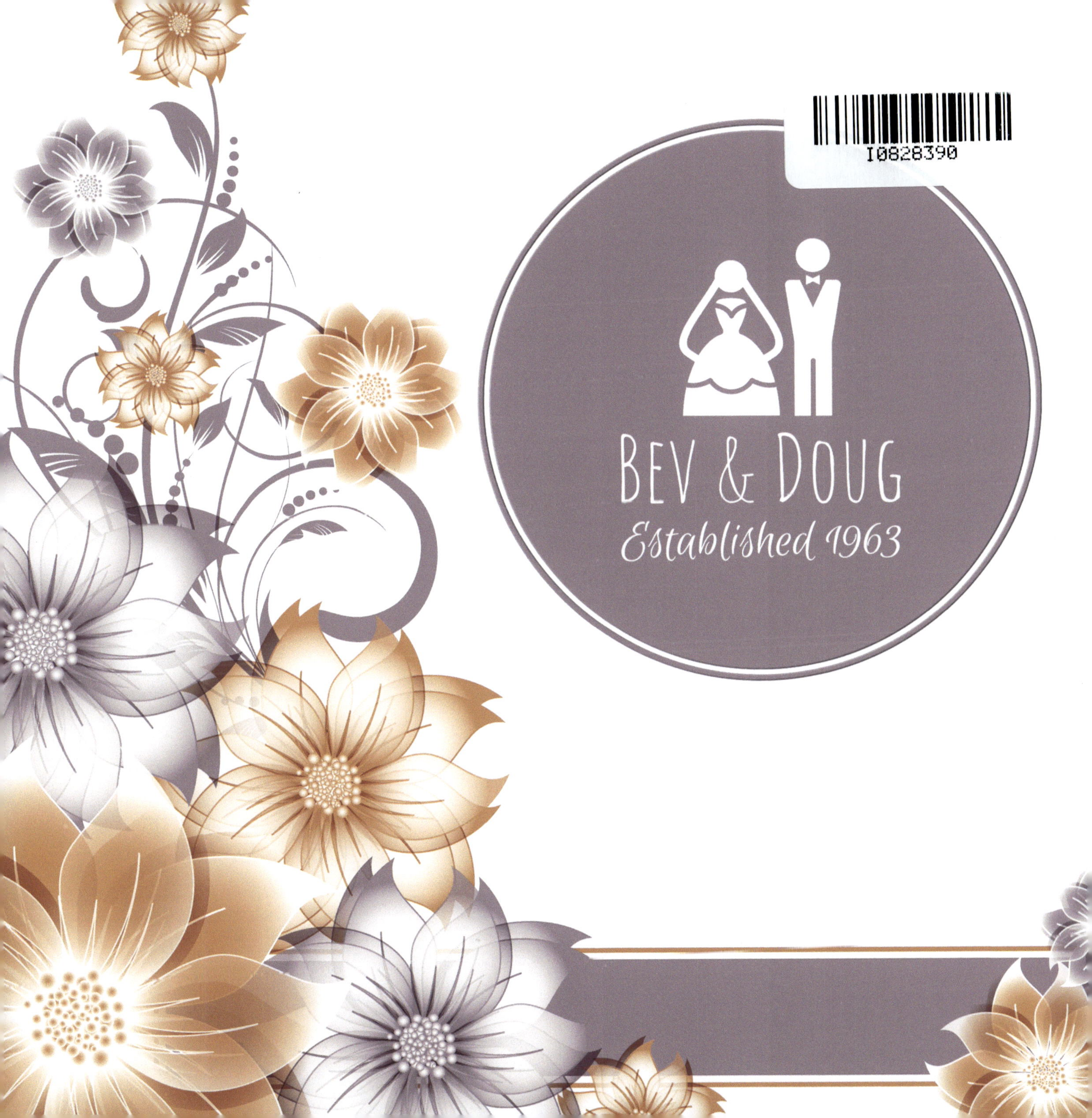
I0828390
BEV & DOUG
Established 1963

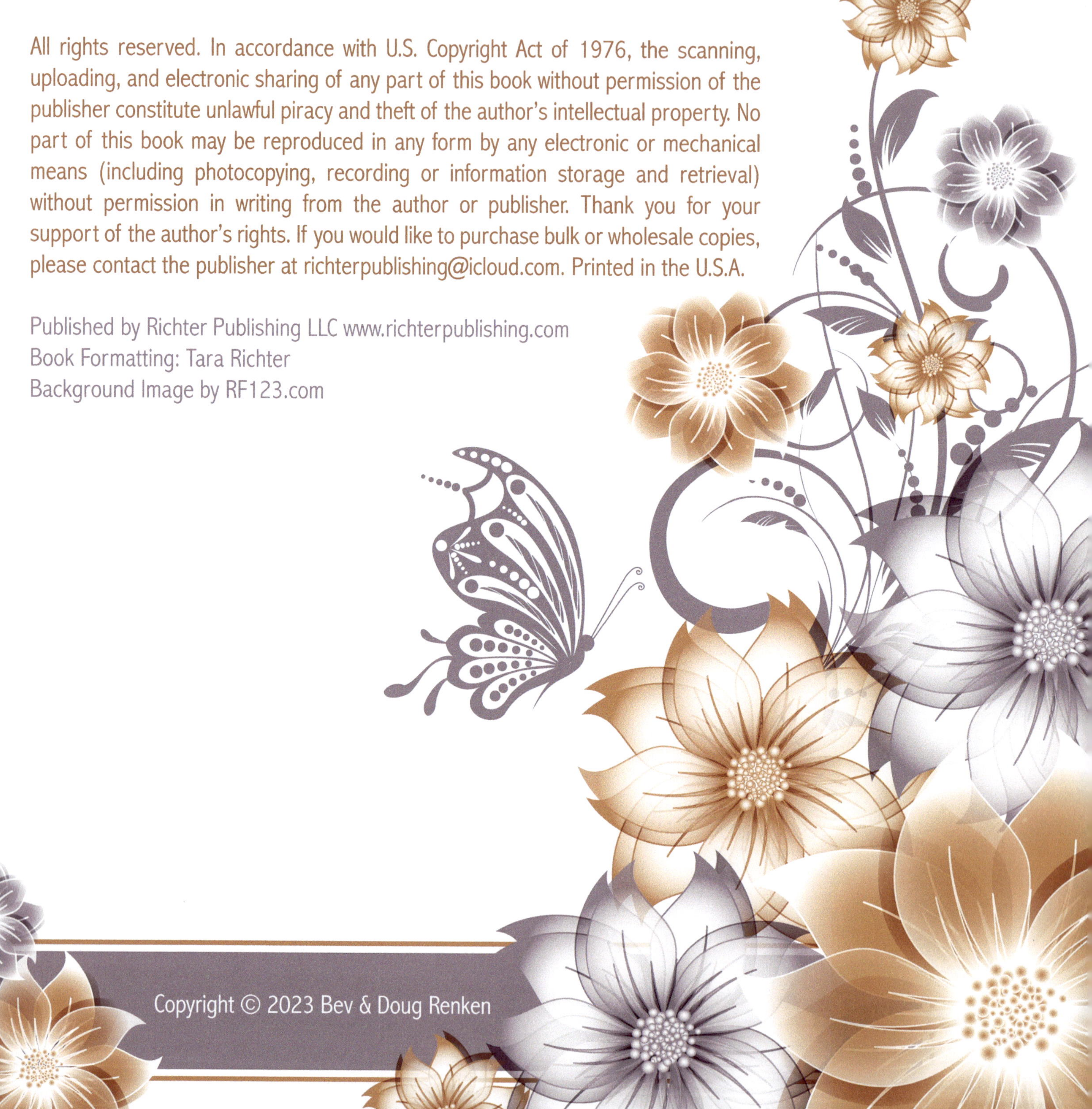

Published by Richter Publishing LLC www.richterpublishing.com
Book Formatting: Tara Richter
Background Image by RF123.com

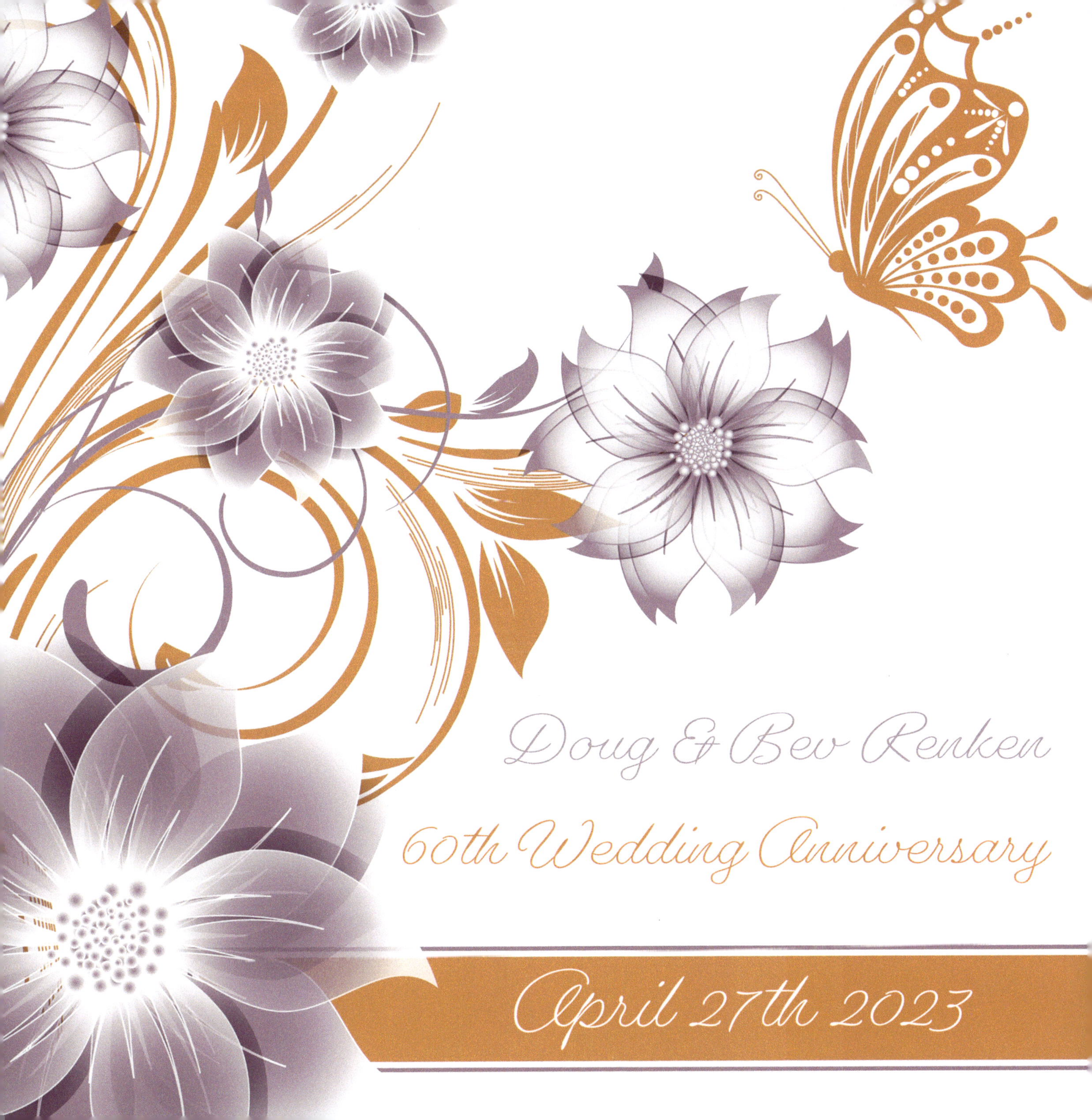
Doug & Bev Renken
60th Wedding Anniversary
April 27th 2023

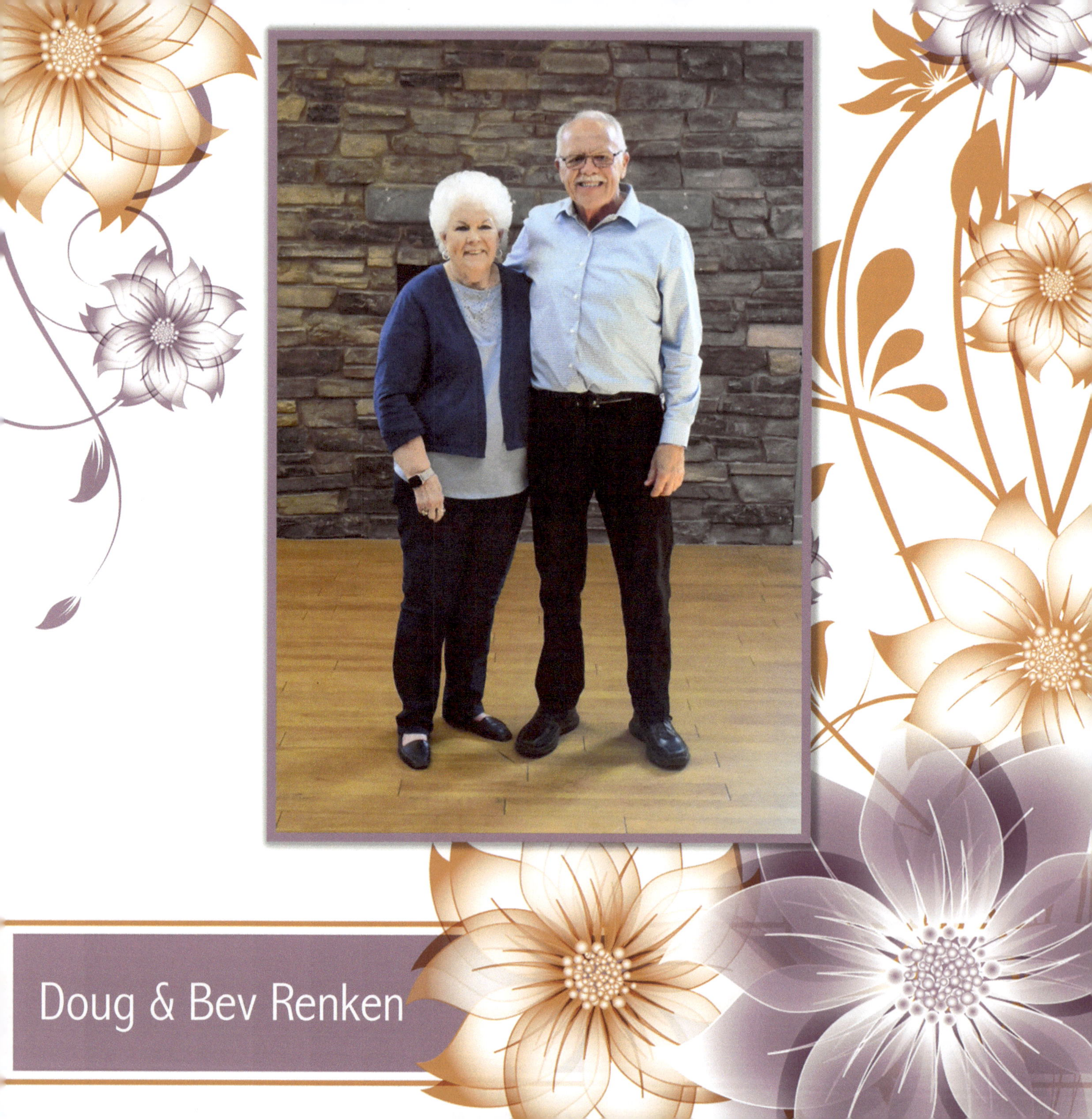

Doug & Bev Renken

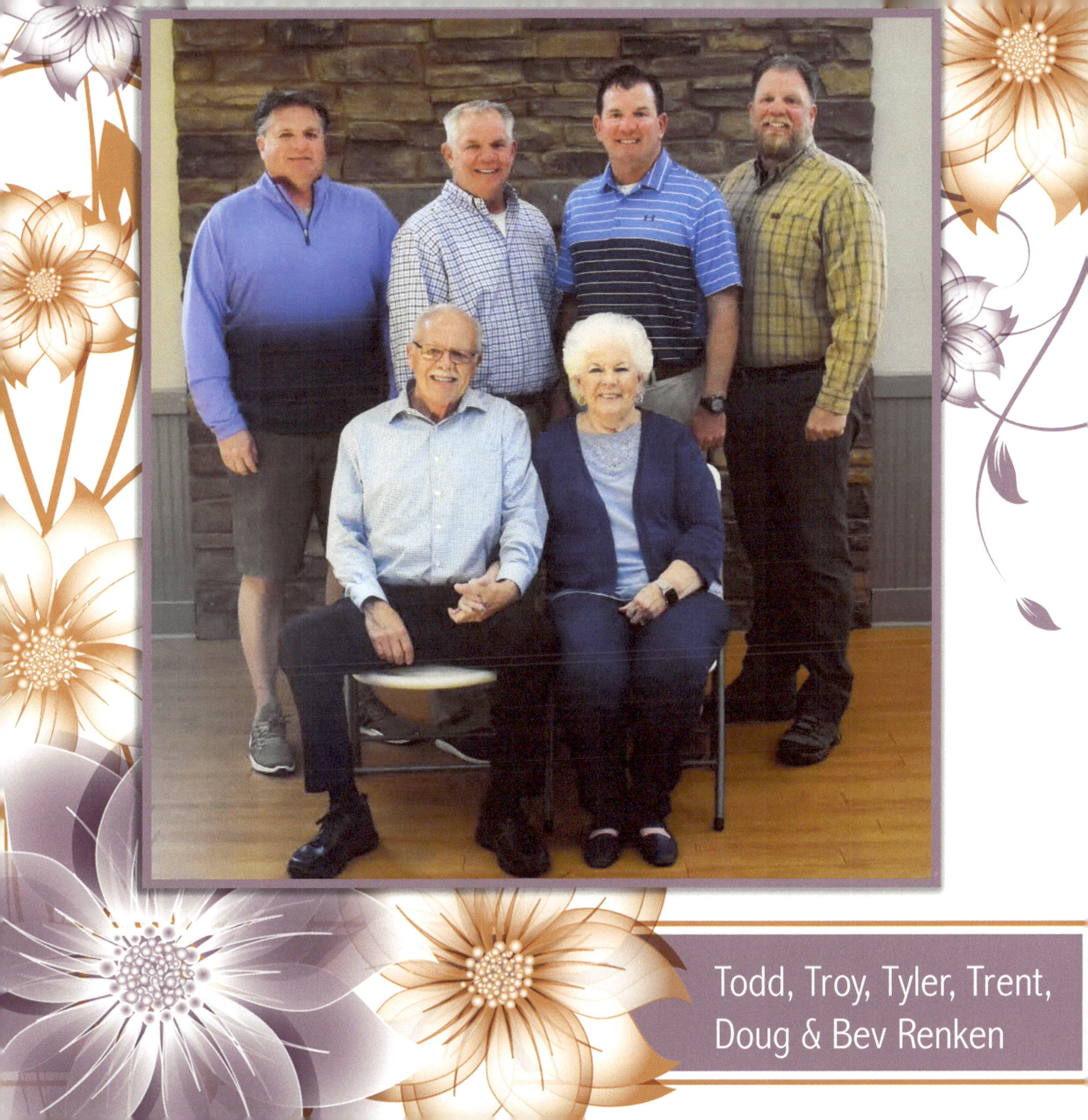

Todd, Troy, Tyler, Trent,
Doug & Bev Renken

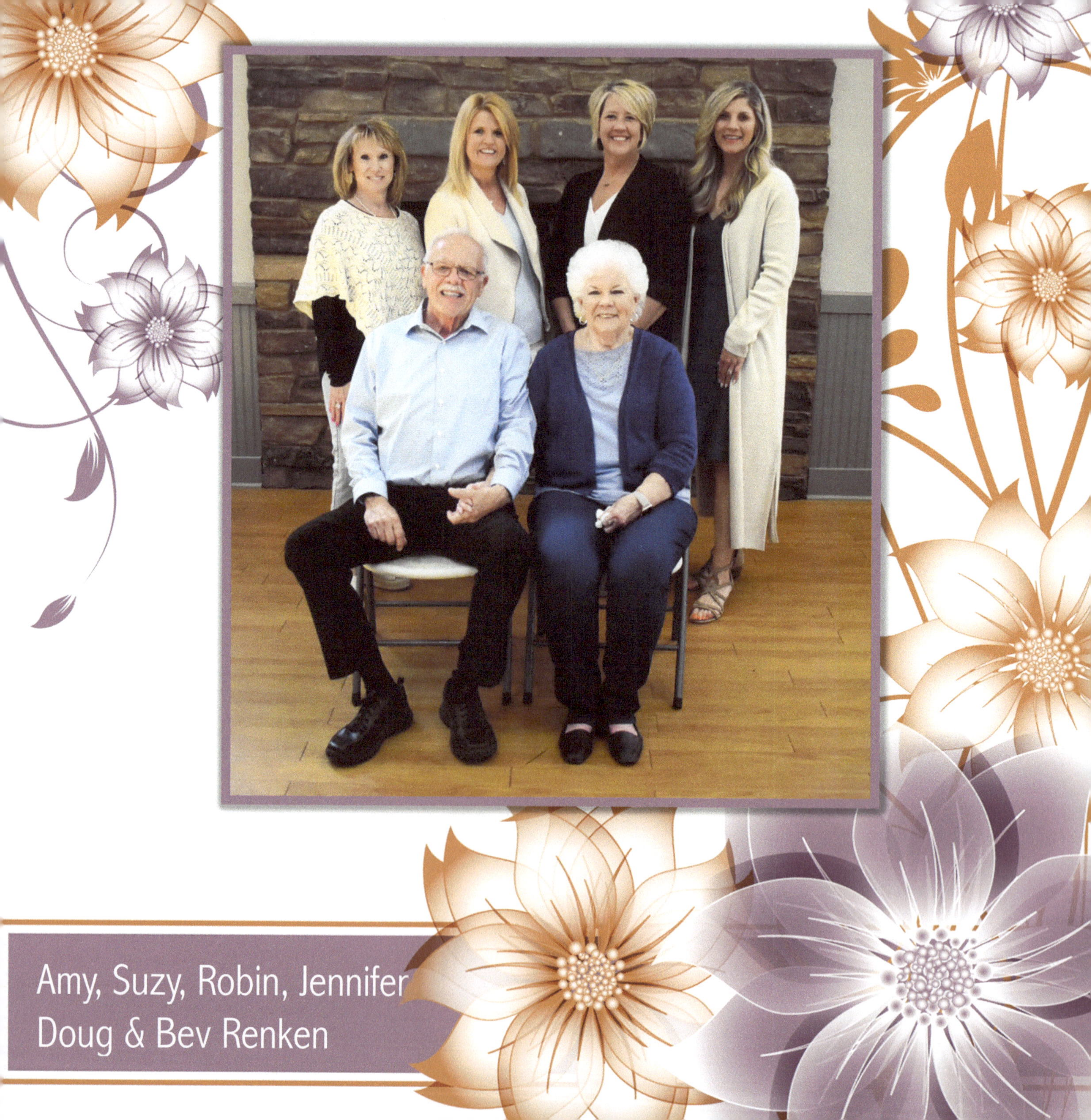

Amy, Suzy, Robin, Jennifer
Doug & Bev Renken

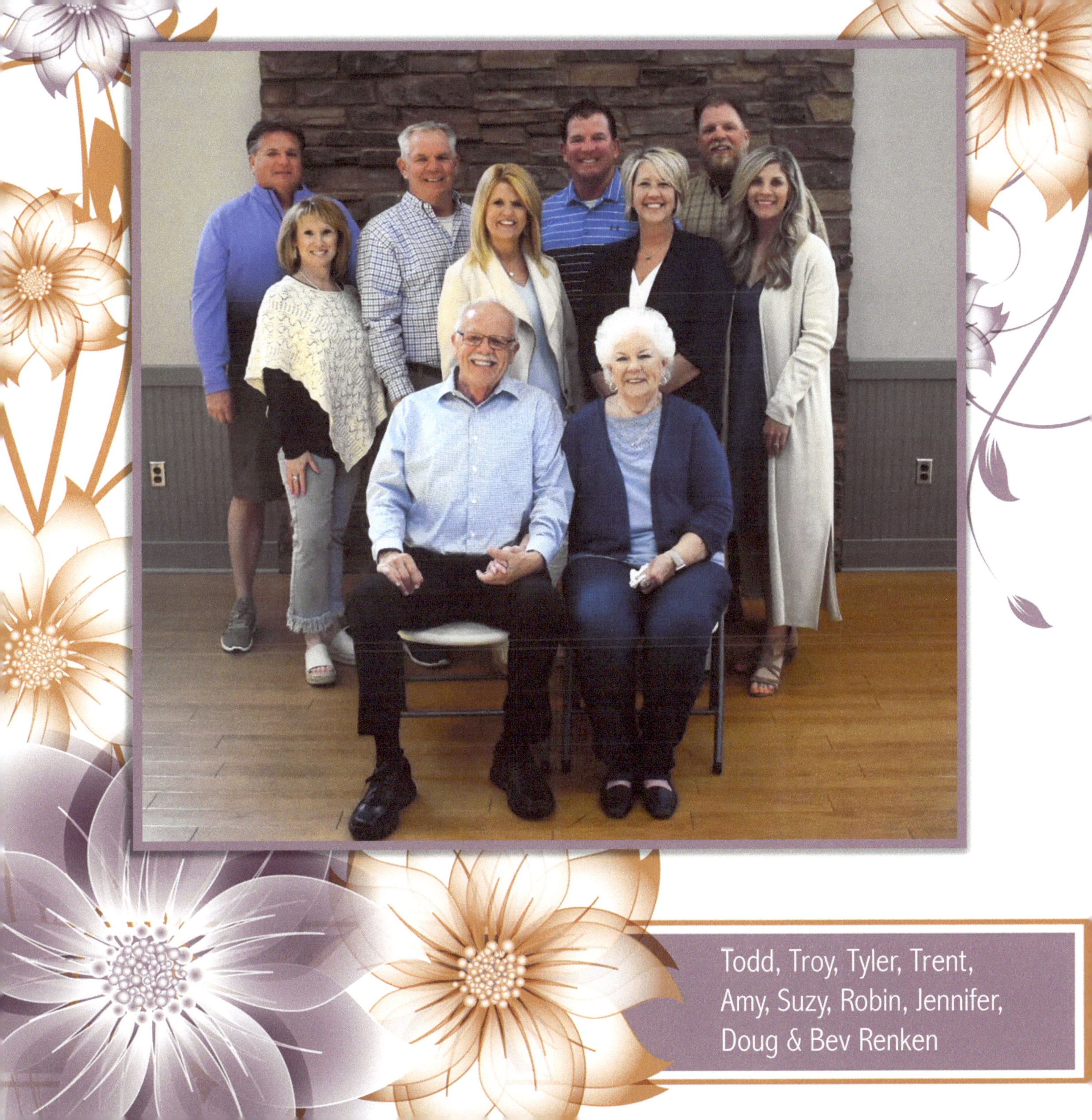

Todd, Troy, Tyler, Trent,
Amy, Suzy, Robin, Jennifer,
Doug & Bev Renken

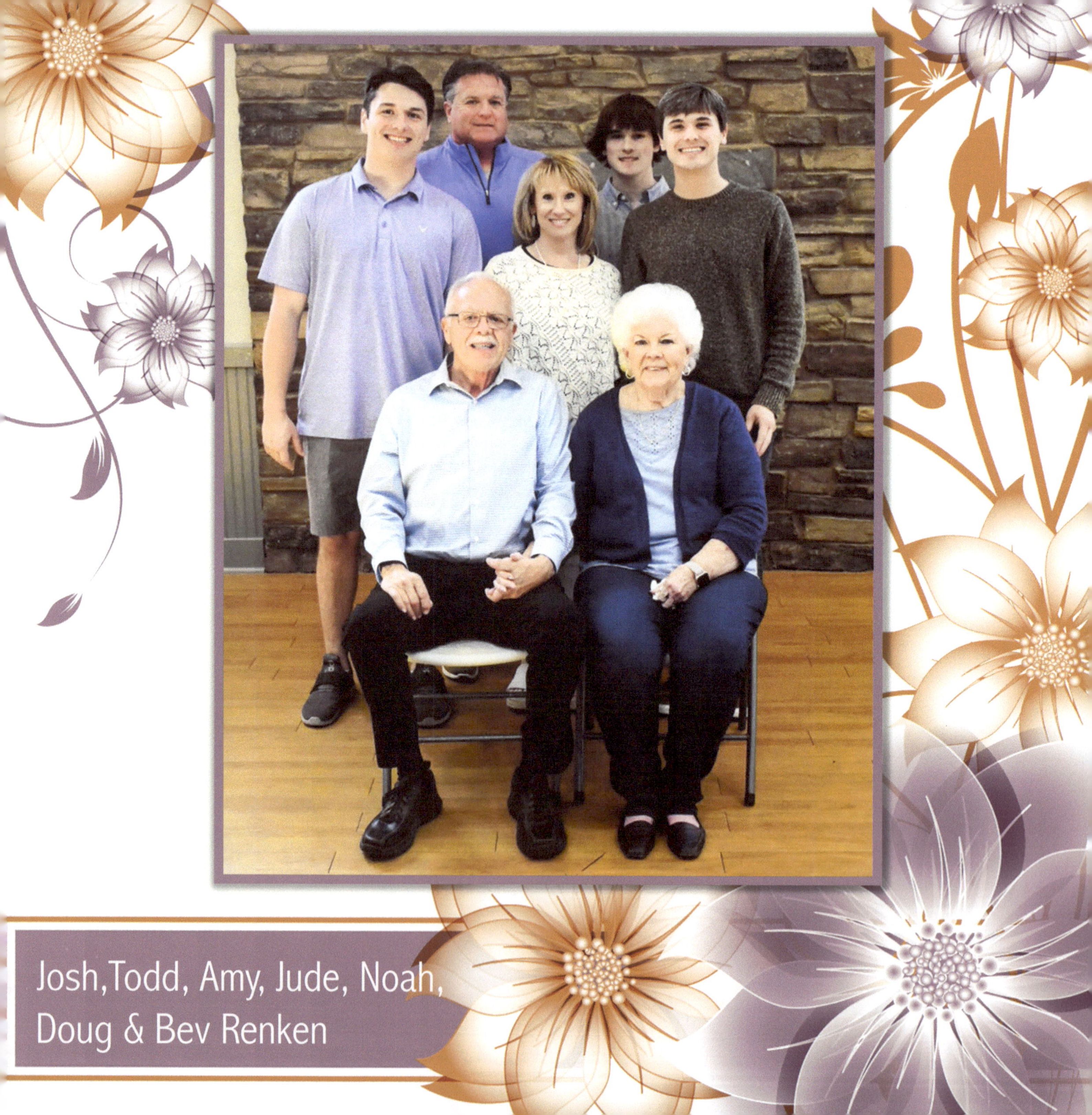

Josh,Todd, Amy, Jude, Noah,
Doug & Bev Renken

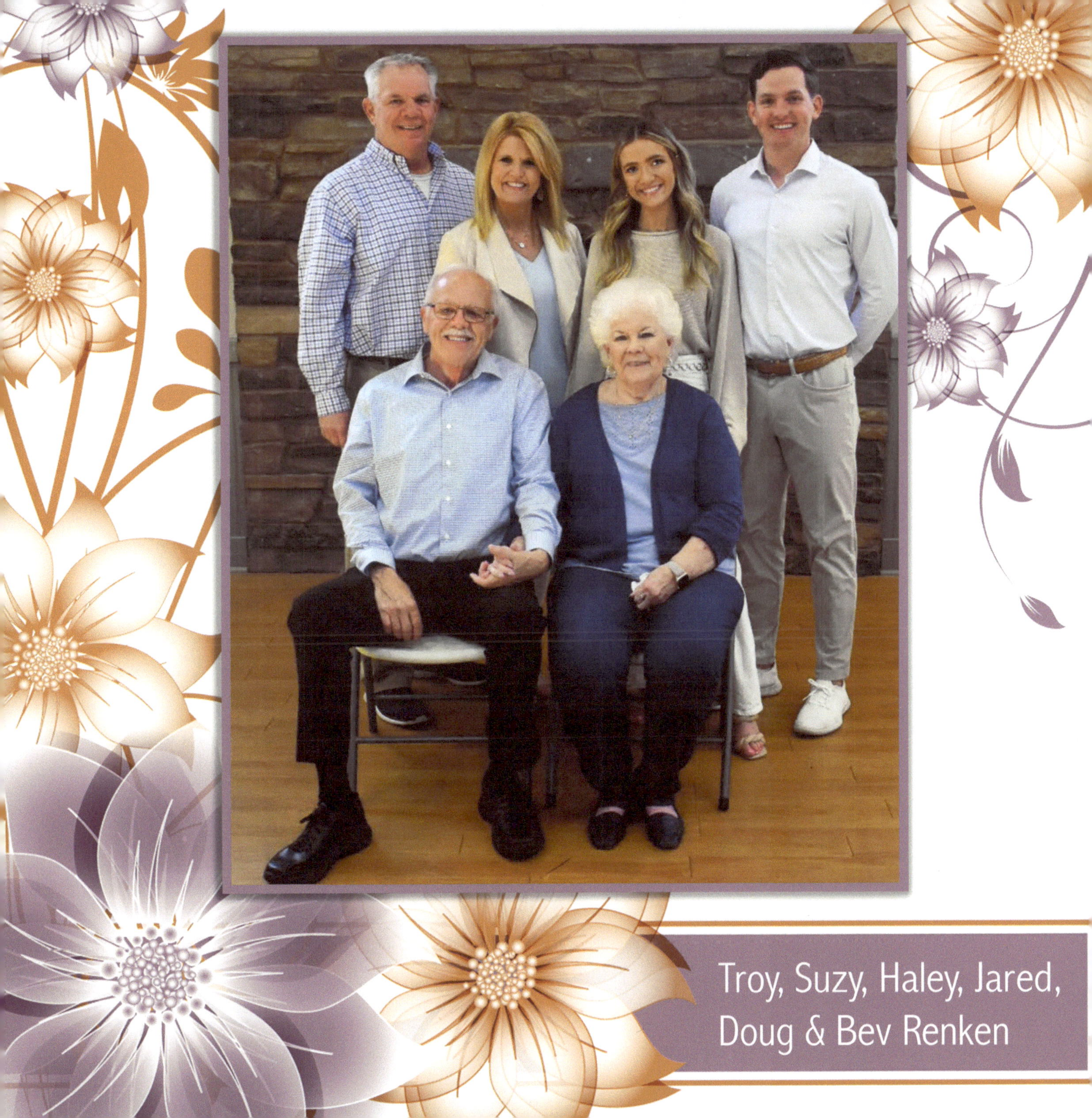

Troy, Suzy, Haley, Jared,
Doug & Bev Renken

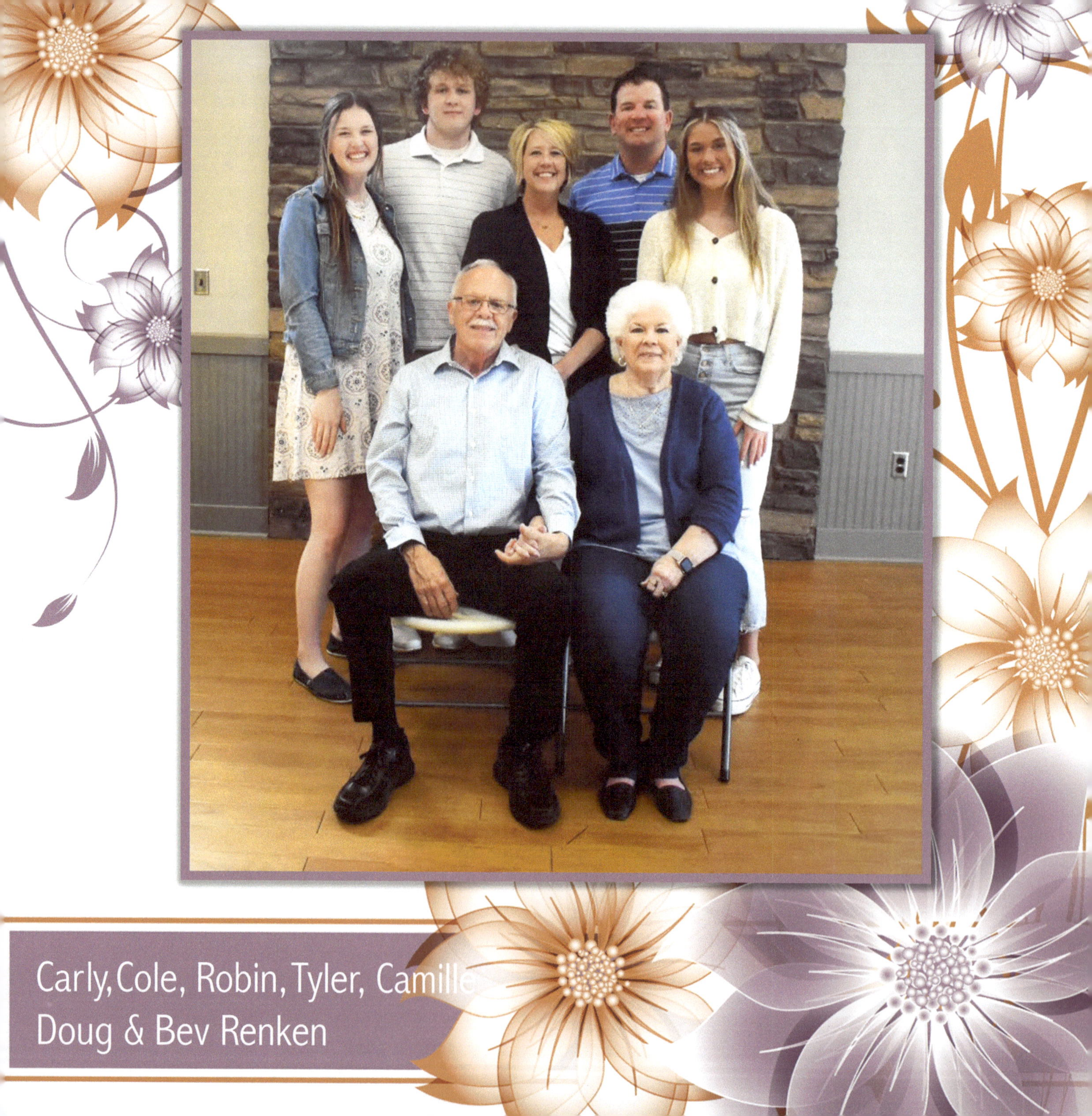

Carly, Cole, Robin, Tyler, Camille
Doug & Bev Renken

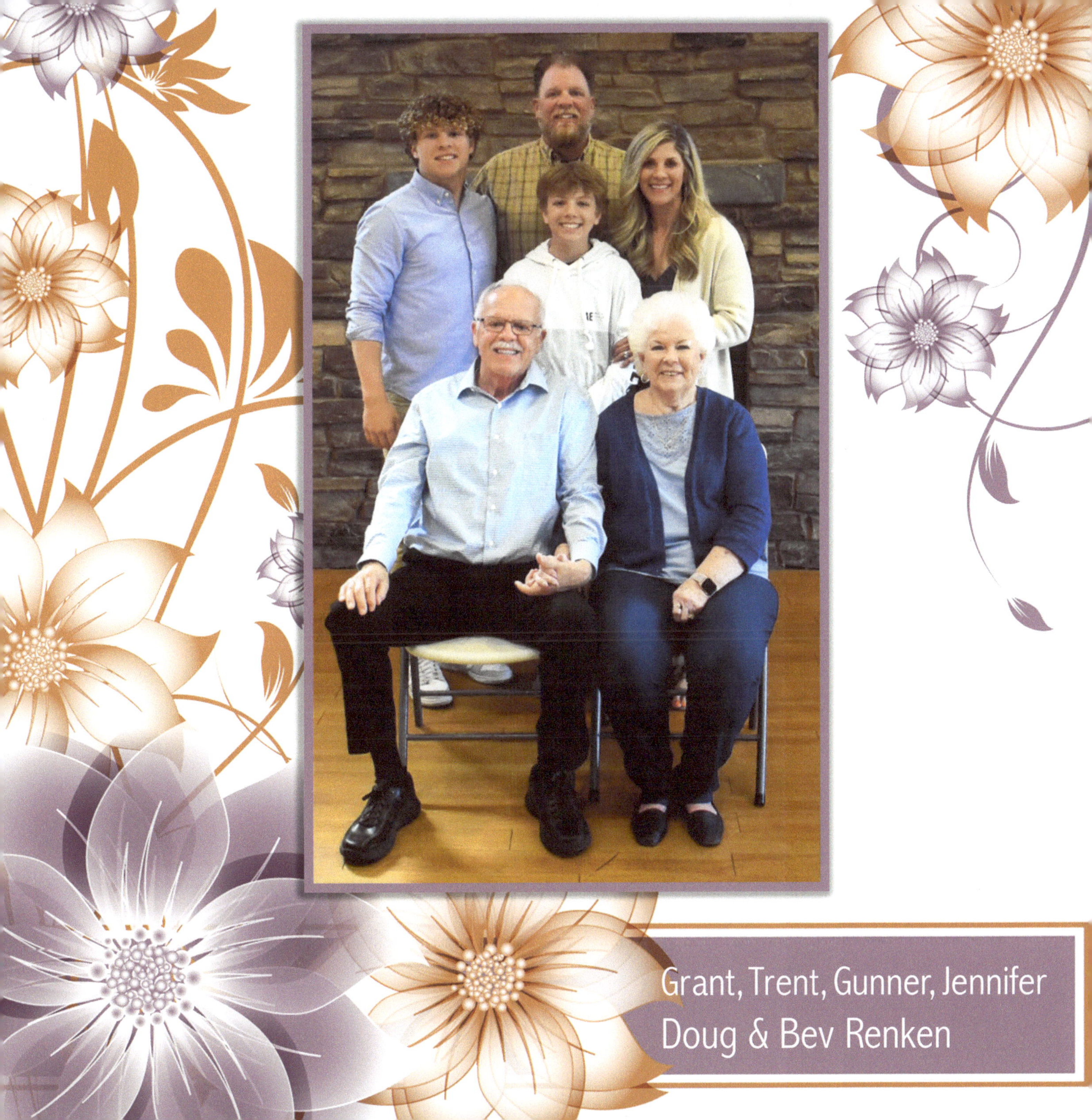

Grant, Trent, Gunner, Jennifer
Doug & Bev Renken

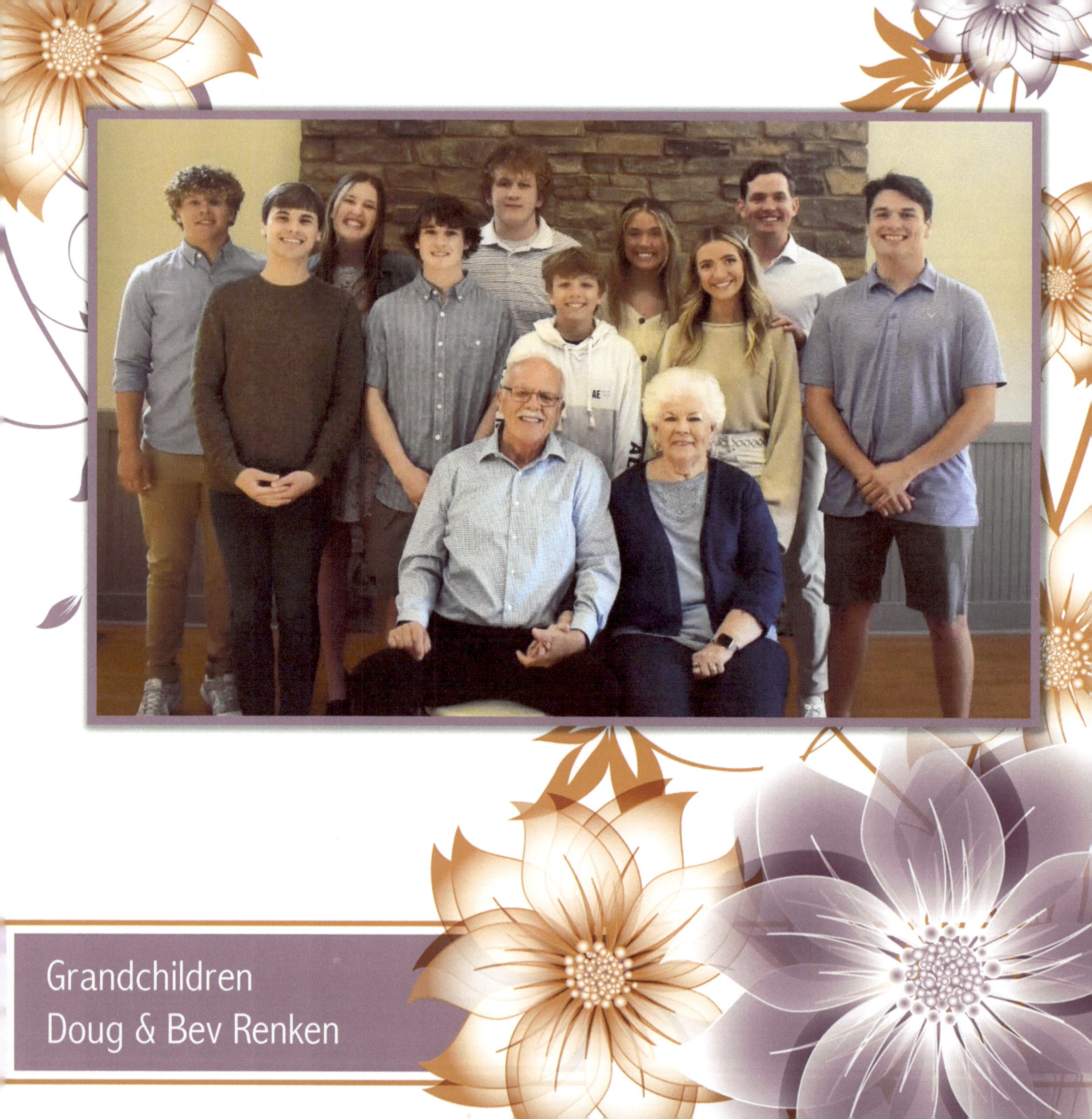

Grandchildren
Doug & Bev Renken

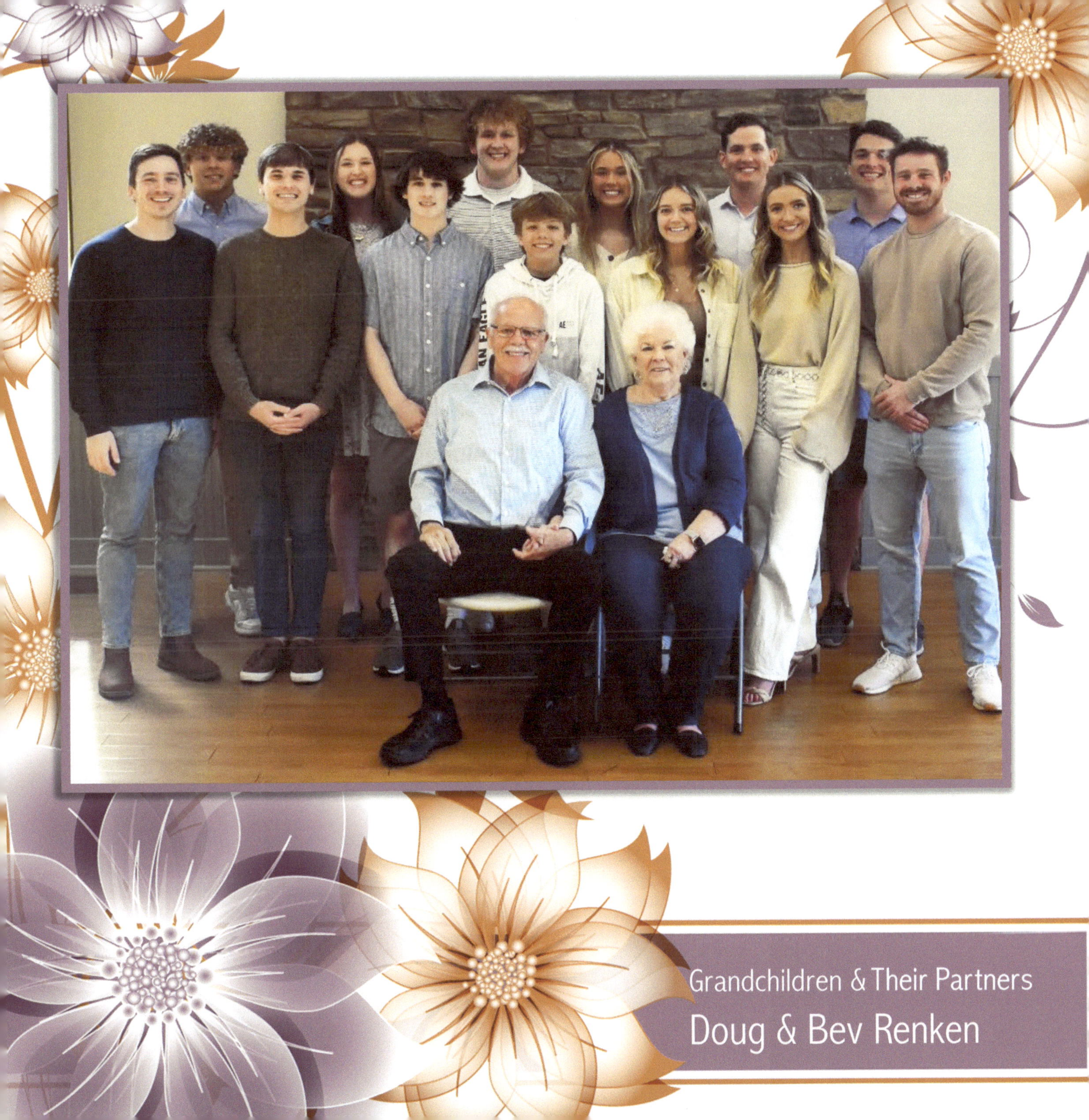

Grandchildren & Their Partners

Doug & Bev Renken

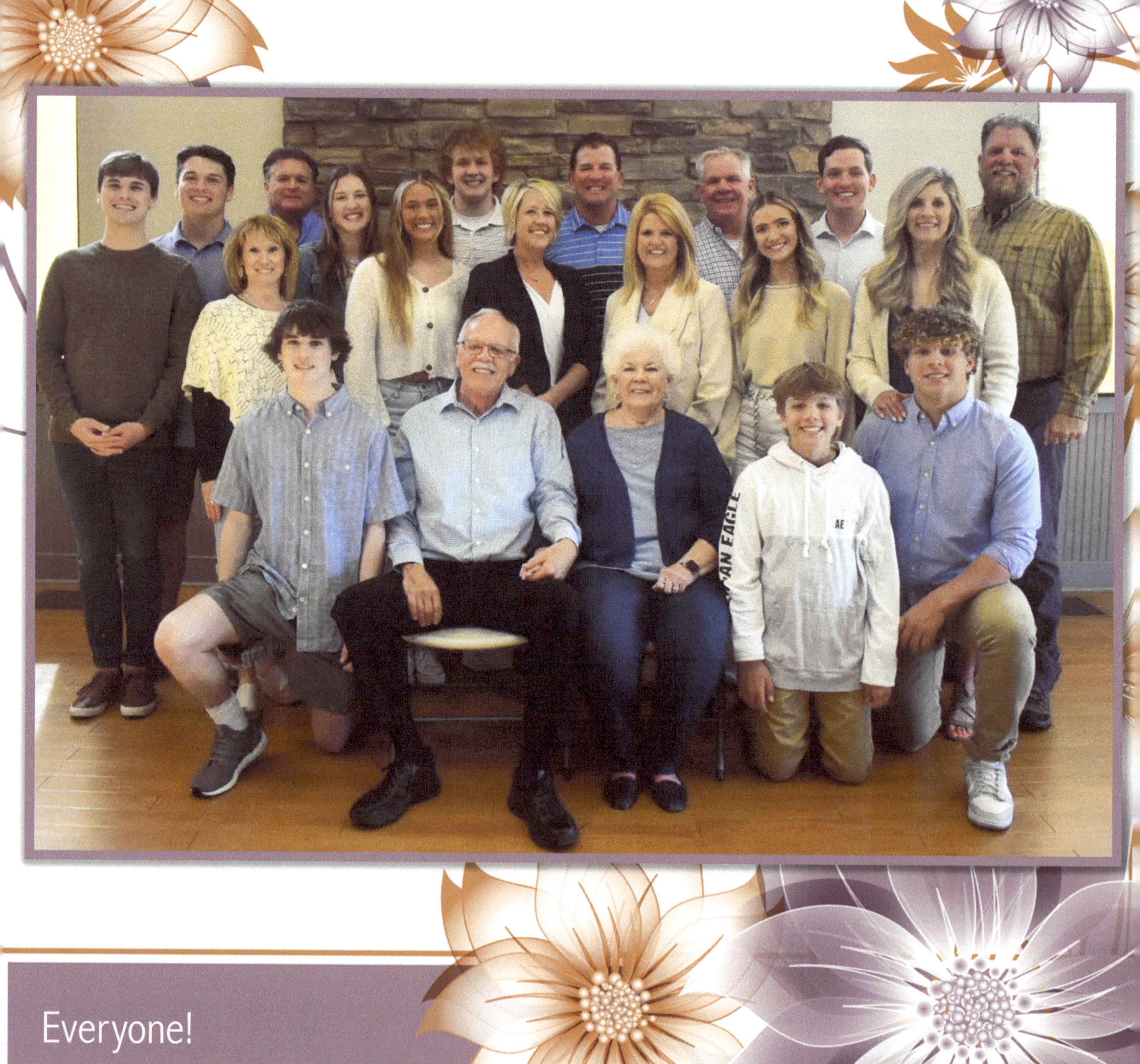

Everyone!

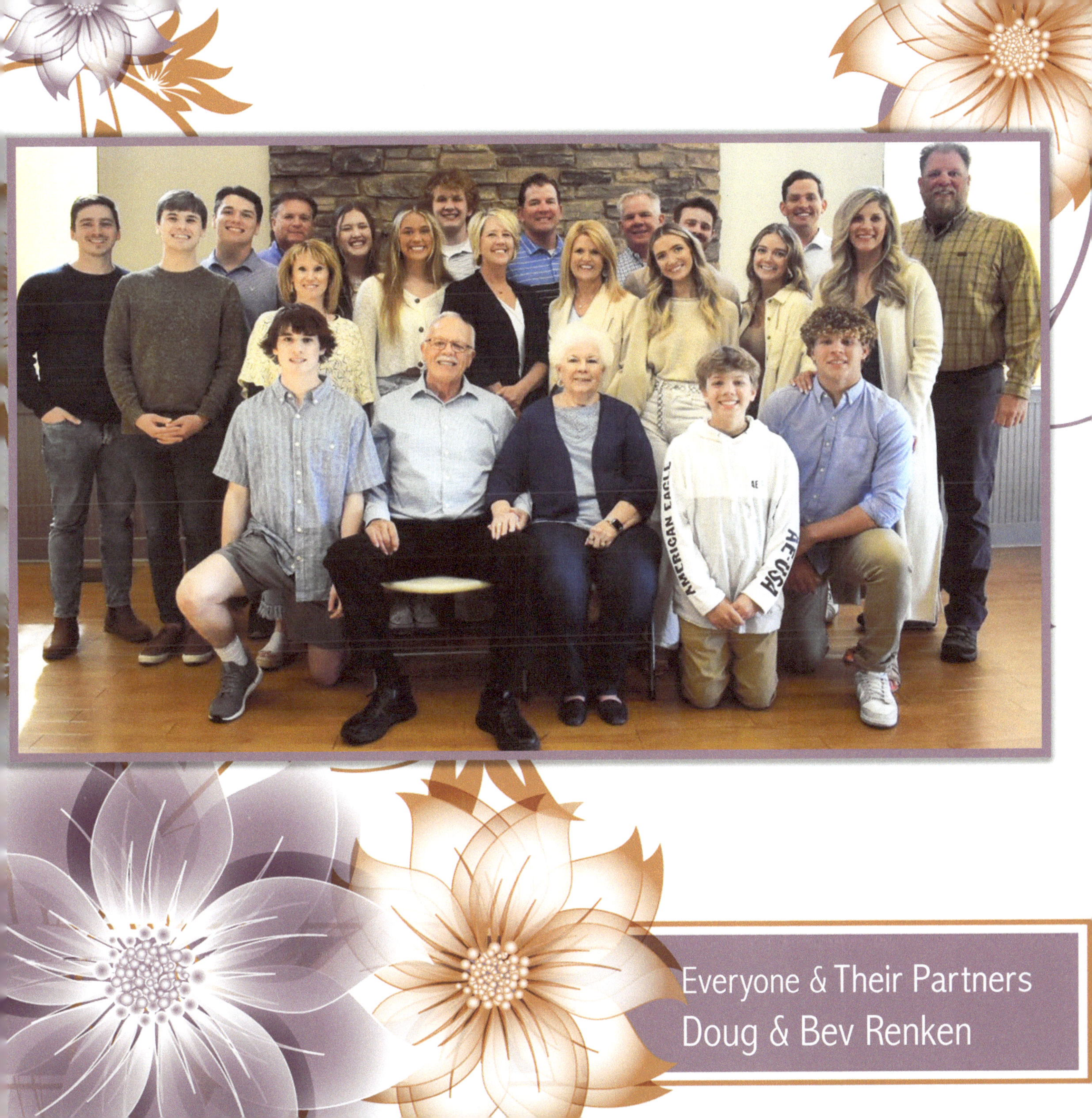

Everyone & Their Partners
Doug & Bev Renken

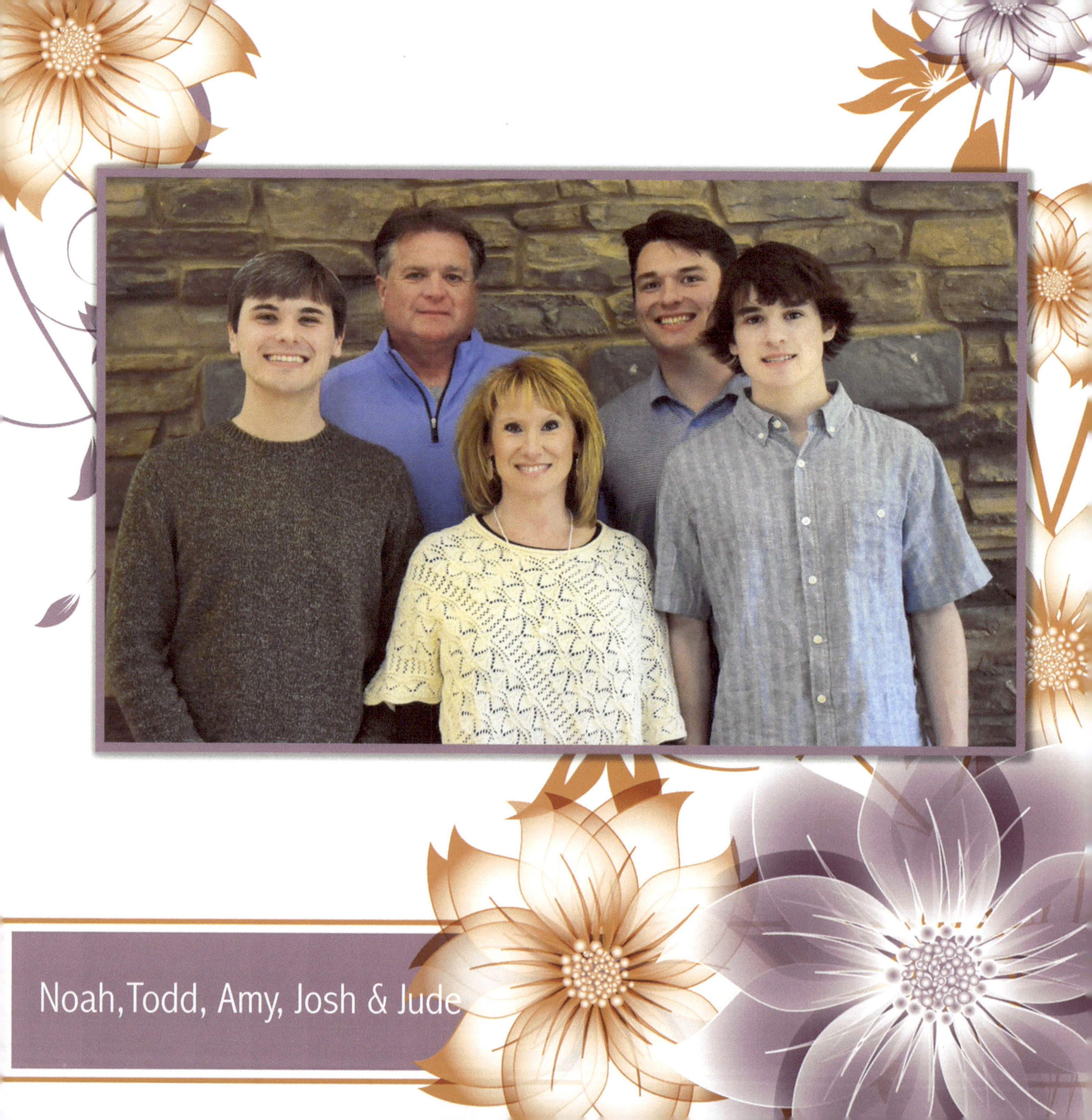
Noah, Todd, Amy, Josh & Jude

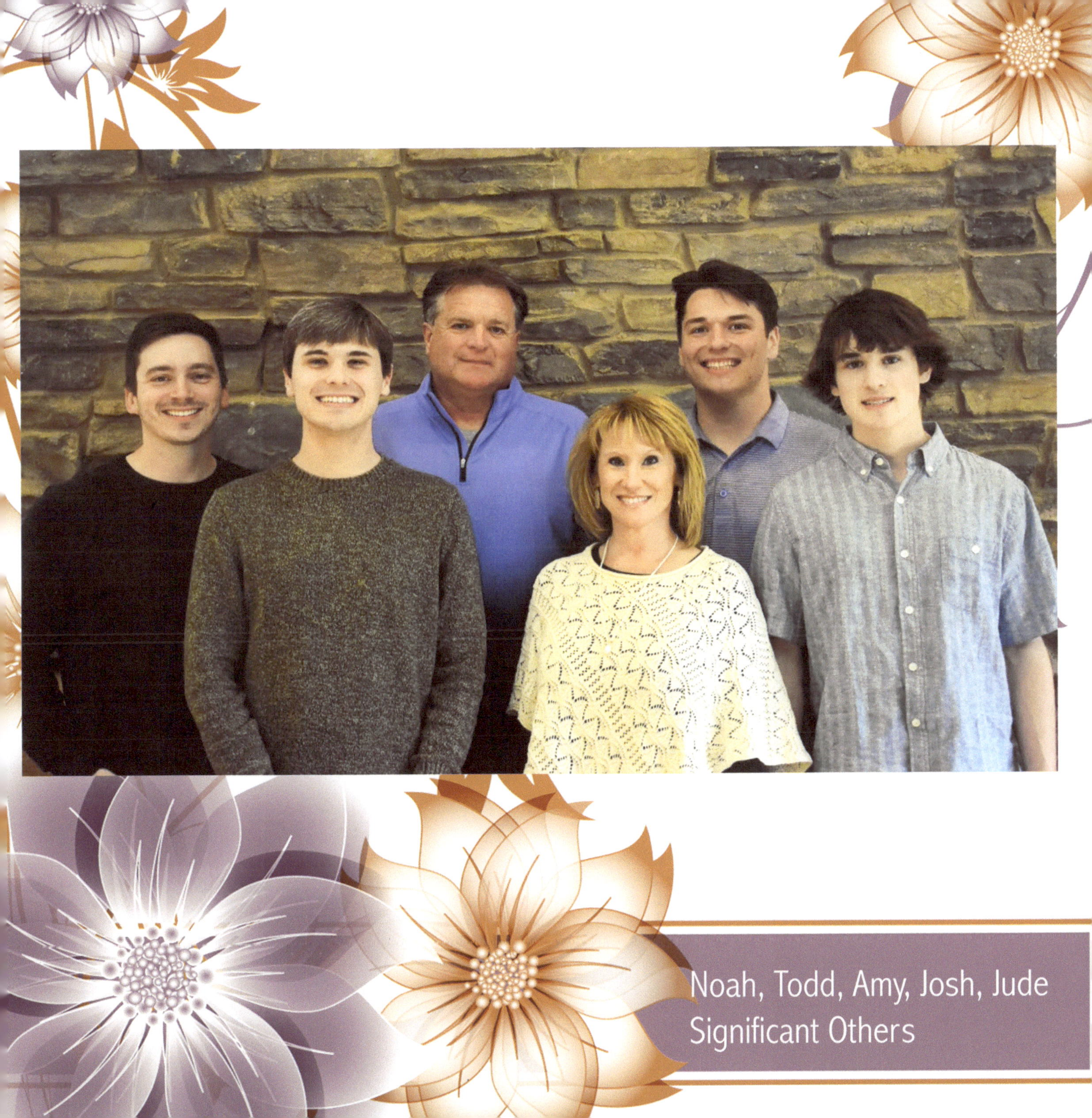

Noah, Todd, Amy, Josh, Jude
Significant Others

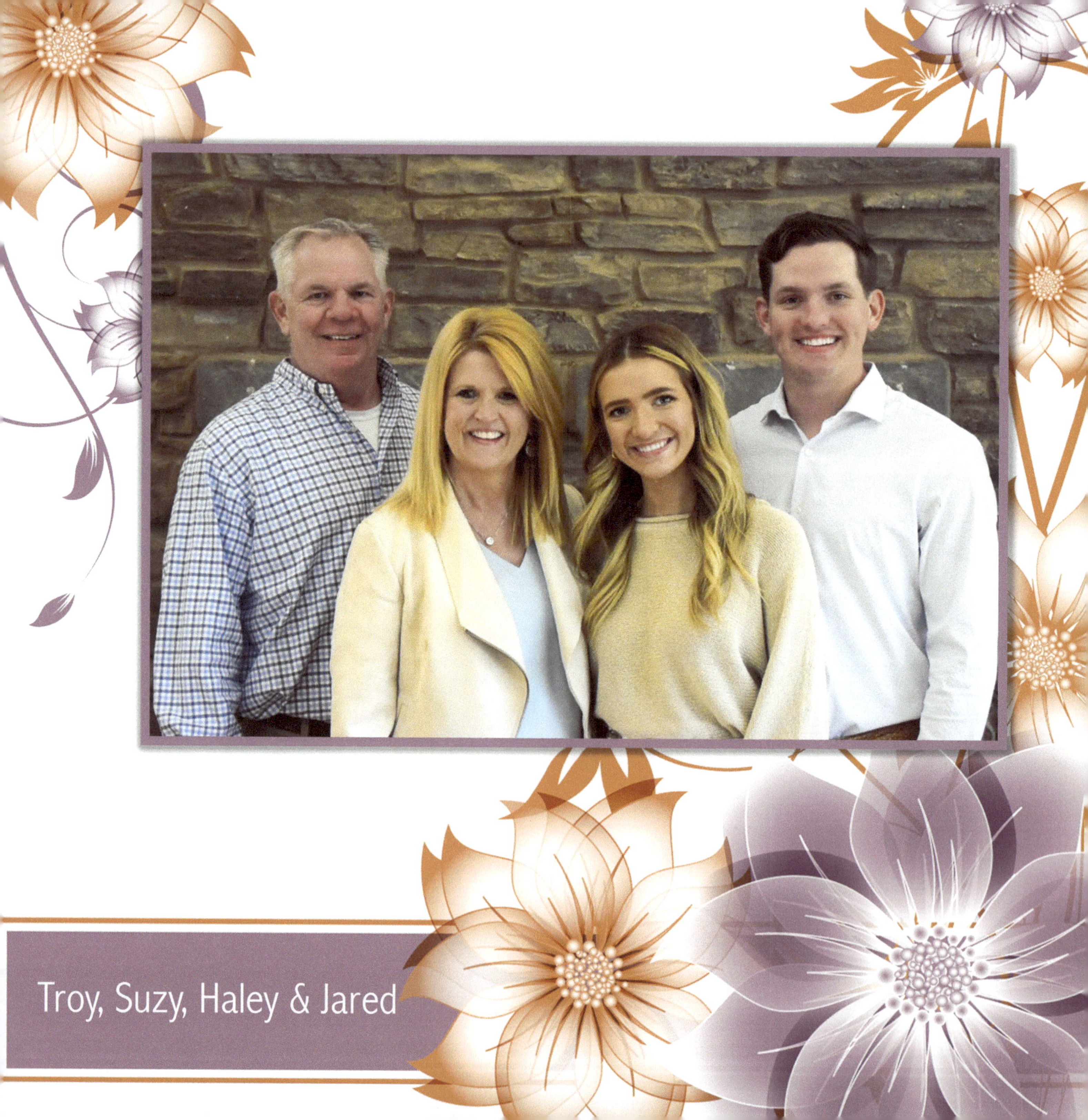
Troy, Suzy, Haley & Jared

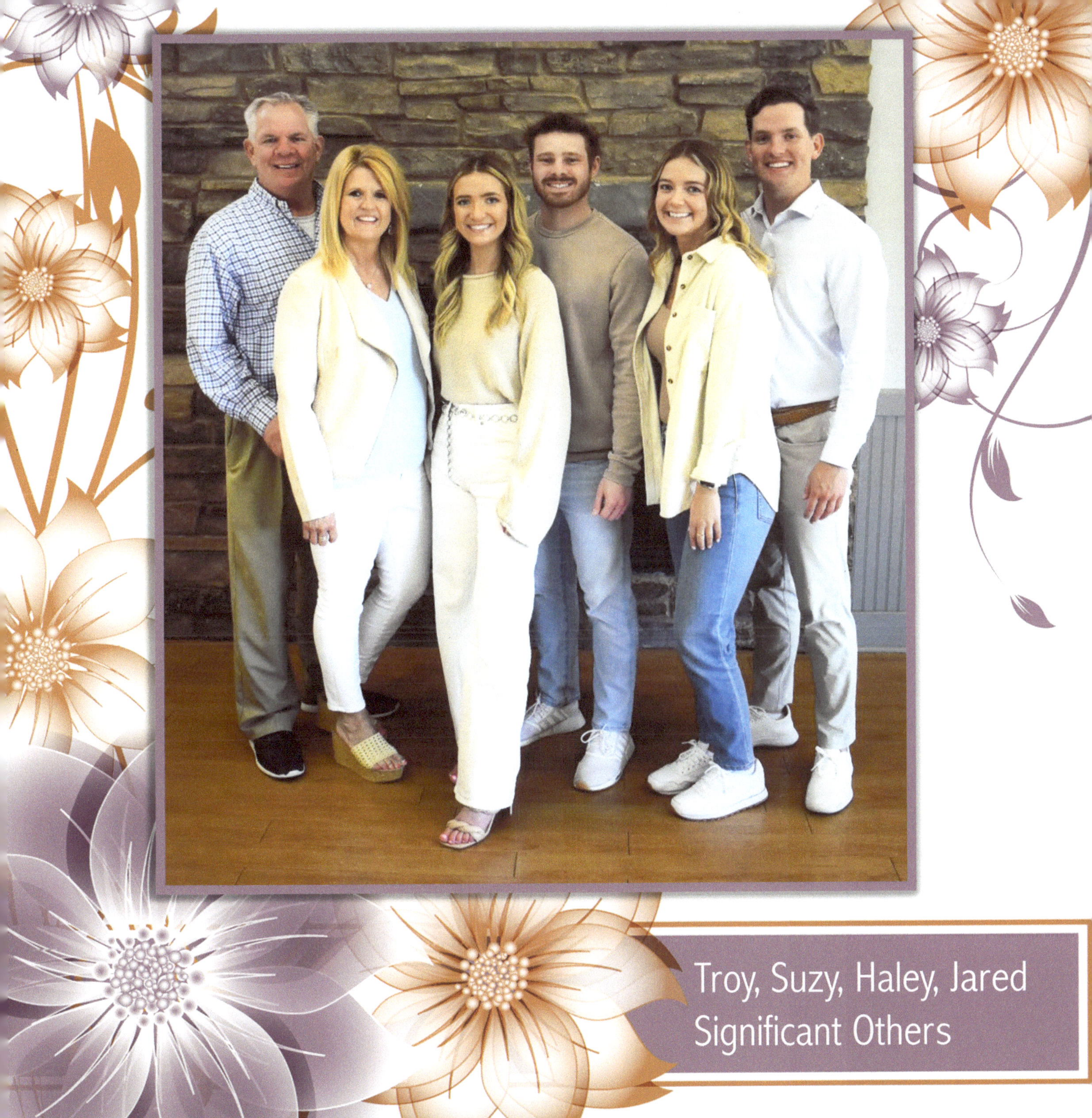

Troy, Suzy, Haley, Jared
Significant Others

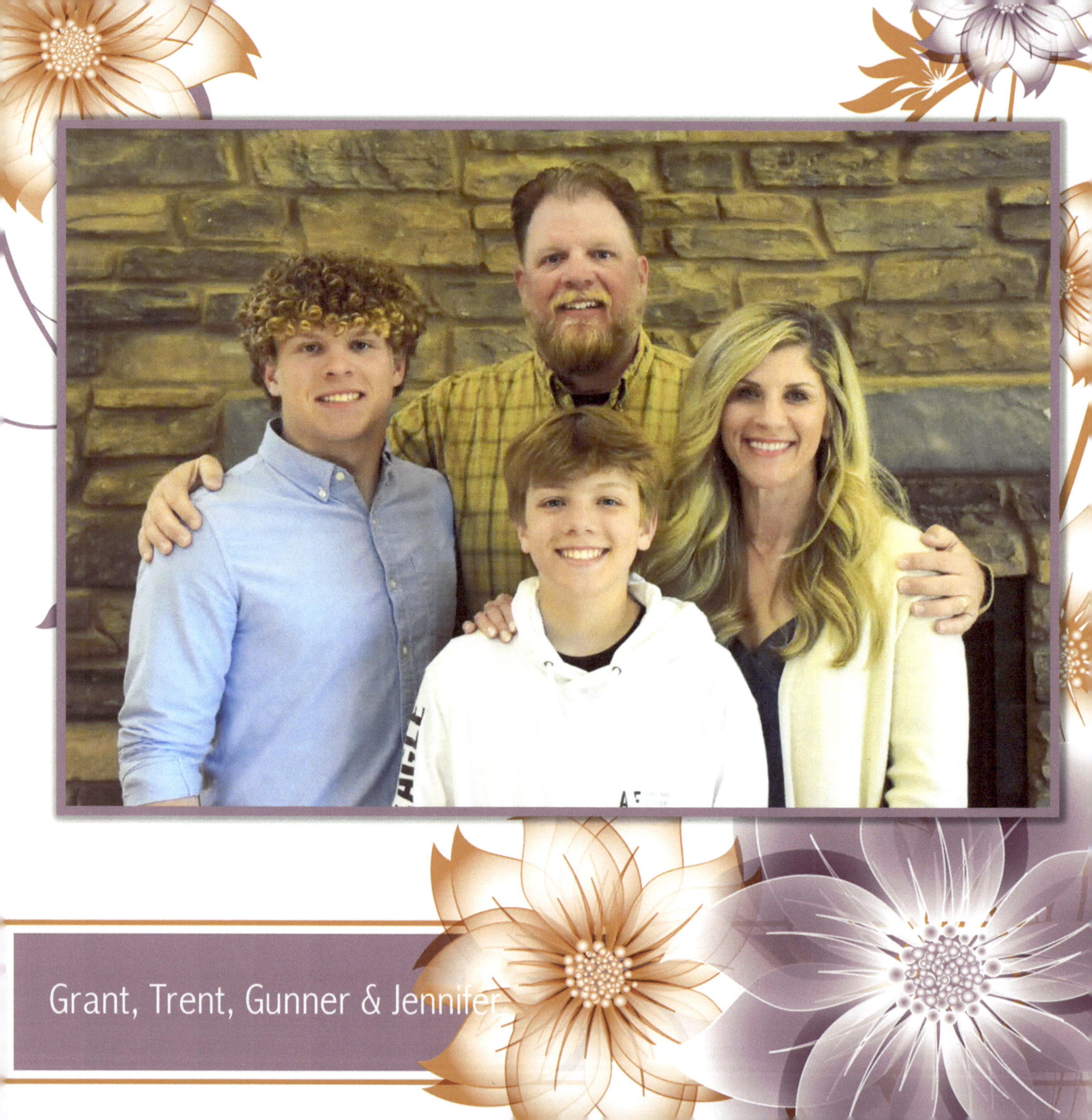

Grant, Trent, Gunner & Jennifer

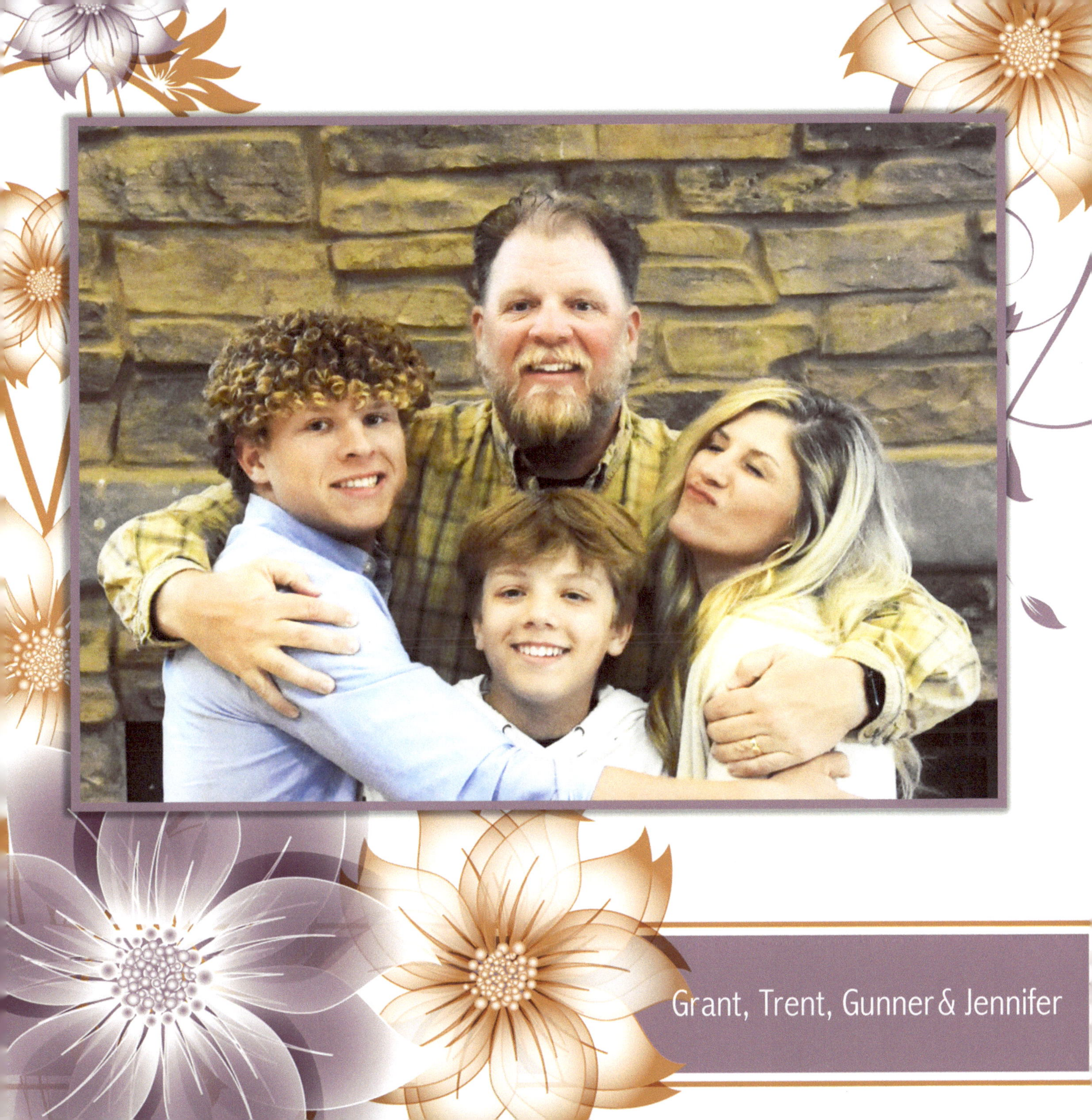

Grant, Trent, Gunner & Jennifer

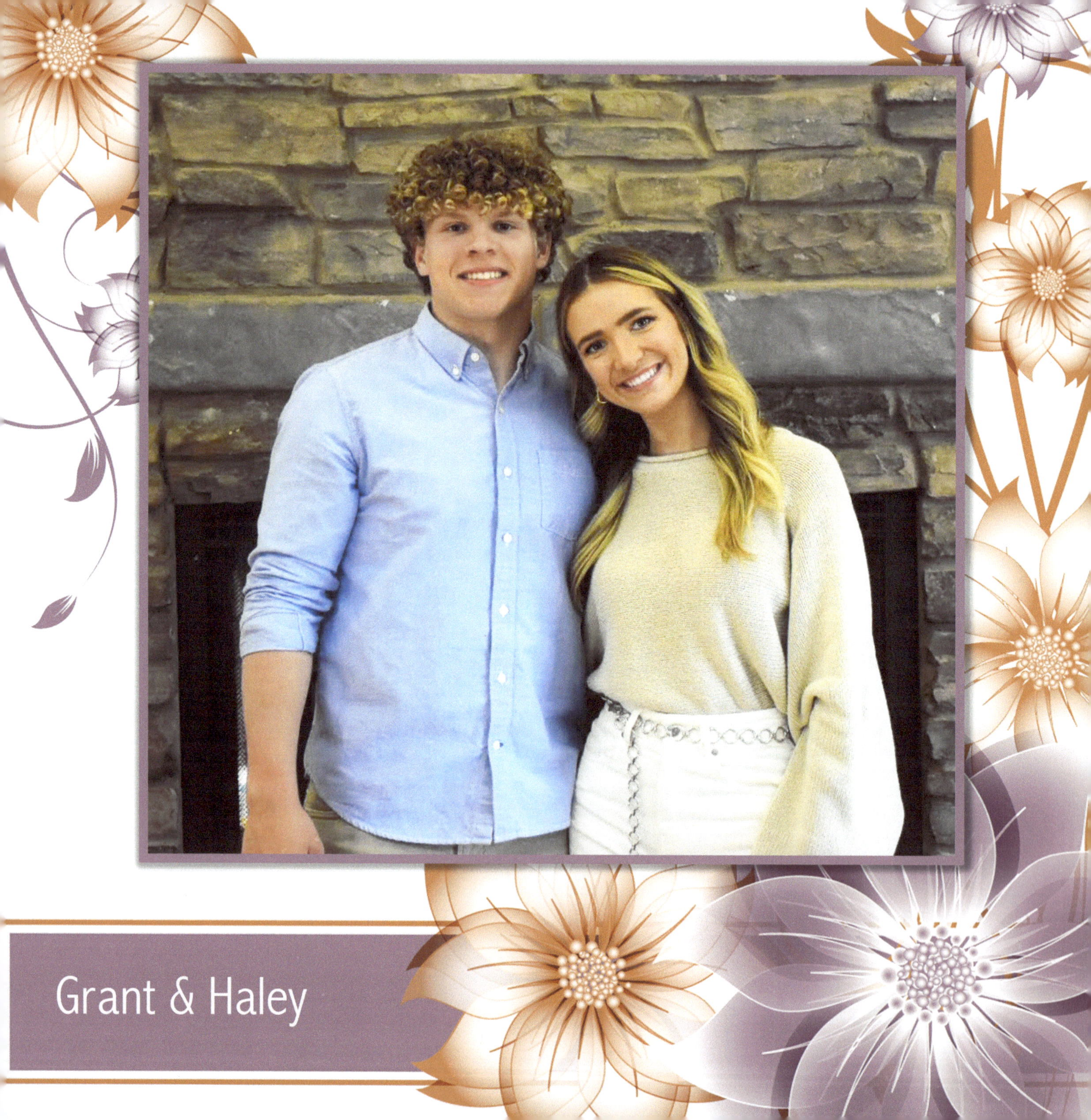
Grant & Haley

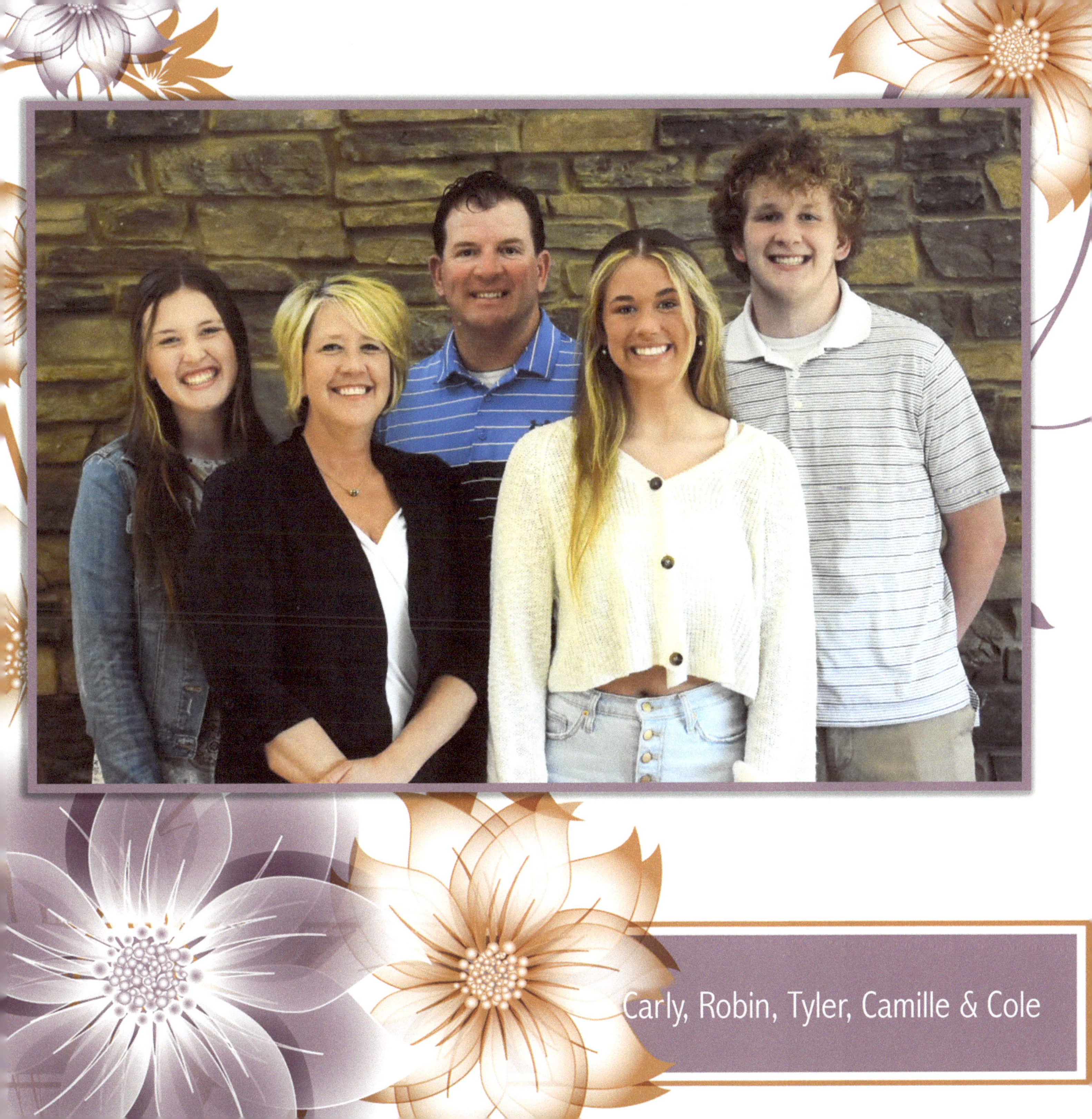

Carly, Robin, Tyler, Camille & Cole

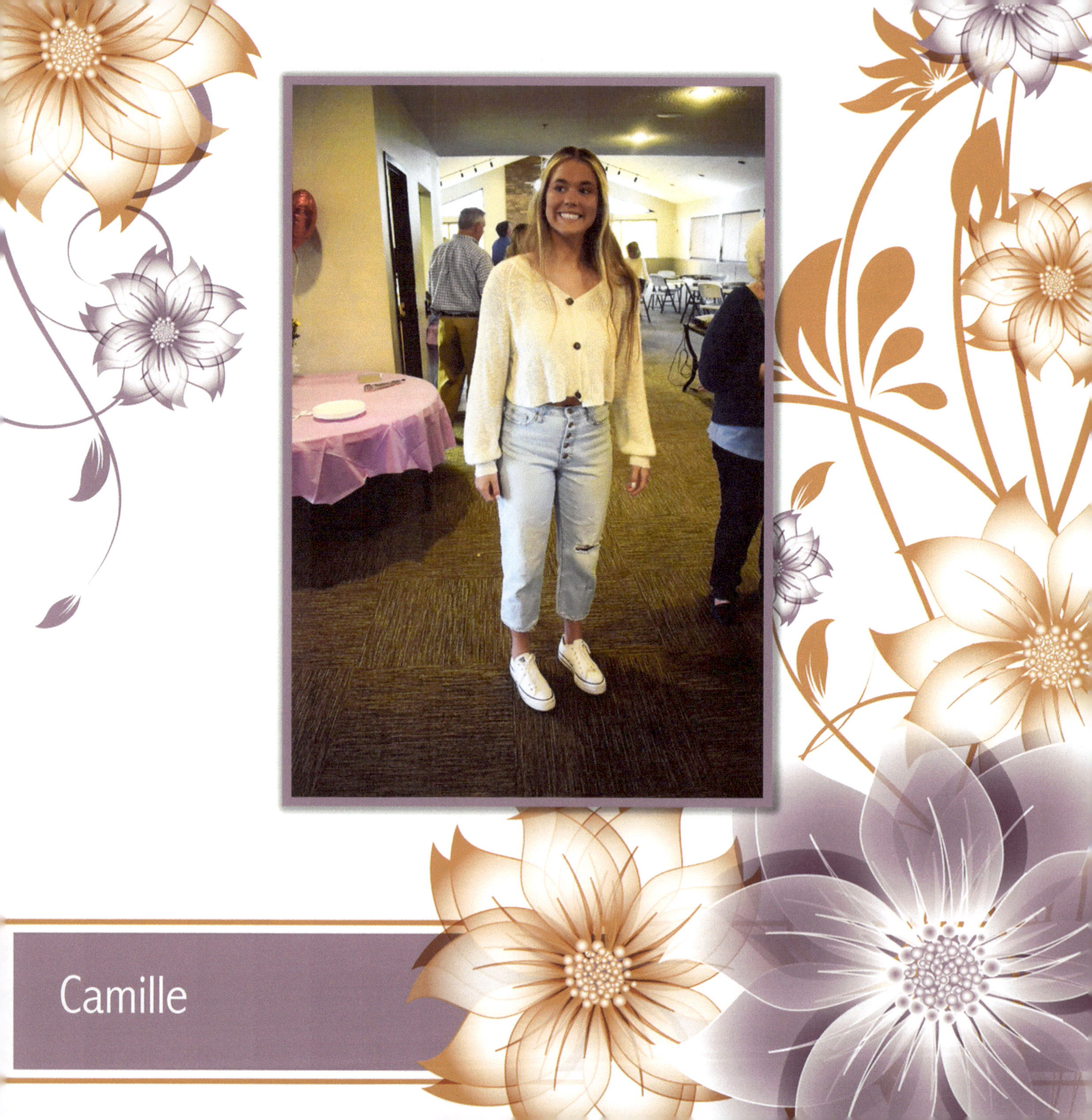
Camille

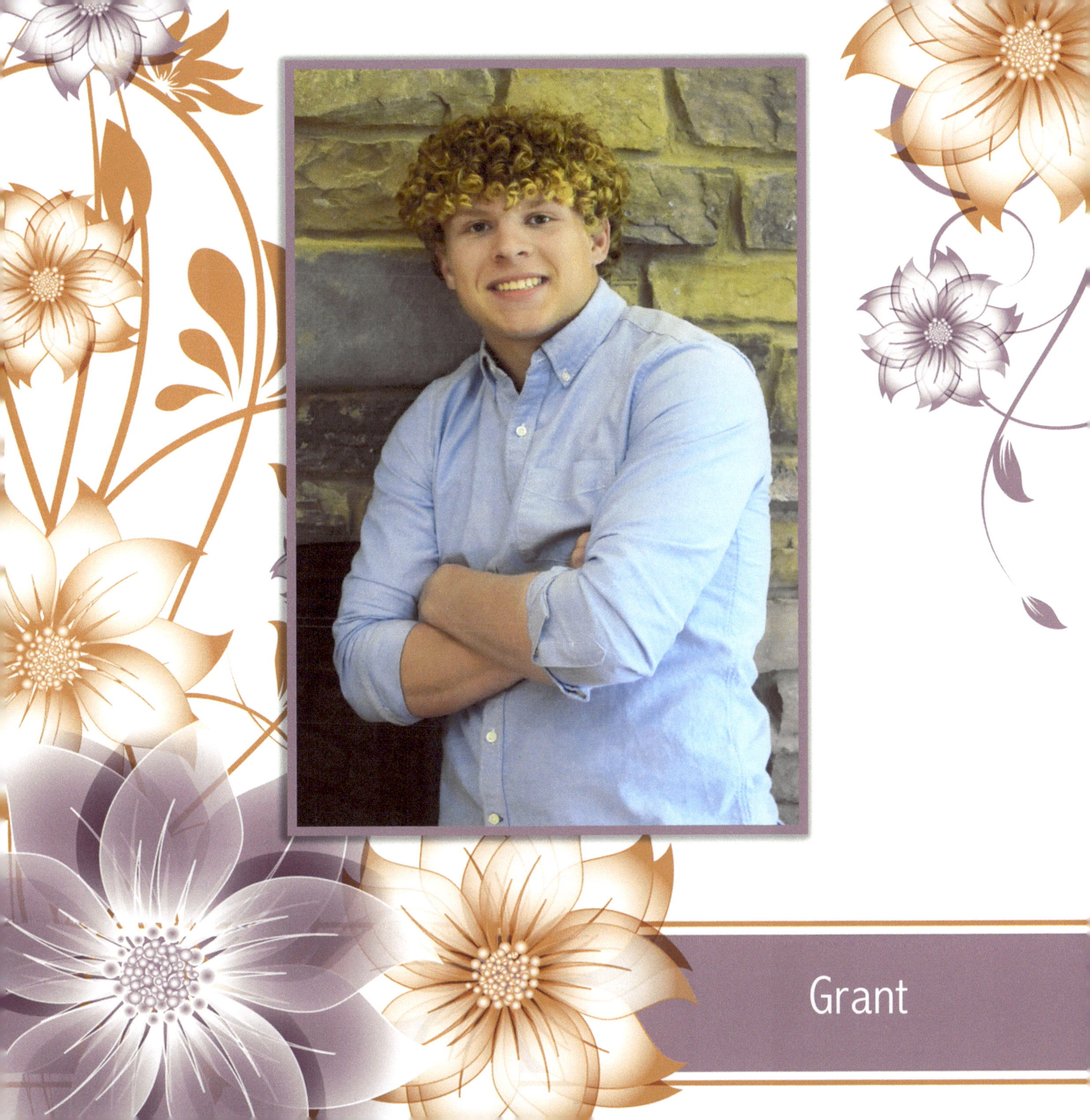
Grant

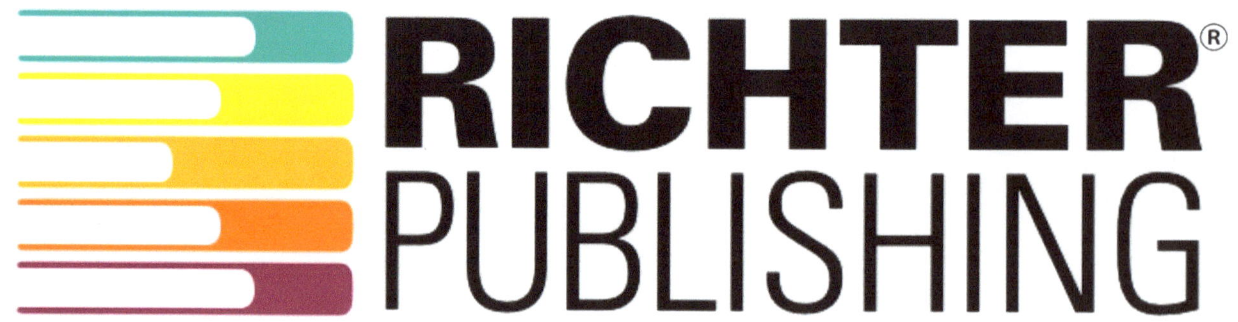
RICHTER®
PUBLISHING